LEARN TO DRAW

Disney

MICKEY MOUSE

and His Friends

Illustrated by John Loter and the Disney Storybook Artists

Walter Foster

Associate Publisher: Elizabeth T. Gilbert
Managing Editor: Rebecca J. Razo
Art Director: Shelley Baugh
Associate Editor: Emily Green
Production Artists: Debbie Aiken, Rae Siebels
Production Manager: Nicole Szawlowski
International Purchasing Coordinator: Lawrence Marquez

7 9 10 8

Table of Contents

The History of Mickey Mouse

Walt Disney often spoke of the importance of a character's appealing personality in capturing the heart of an audience. Mickey Mouse, Minnie Mouse, Donald Duck, Daisy Duck, Goofy, and Pluto embody this concept, making them the very foundation of the Disney organization—in the beginning and today.

It all started in 1928 when Walt Disney and his small studio were on the verge of losing everything. To recover, Walt needed a new character that was sure to be a winner. In a flash of inspiration, Mickey Mouse was born.

The friendly, fun-loving, and mischievous Mickey Mouse debuted alongside Minnie Mouse in *Steamboat Willie,* the first, fully synchronized sound cartoon. Rave reviews and endless enthusiasm from audiences made Mickey Mouse a superstar overnight. Within weeks, he was a national craze. And by the end of 1930, Mickey was an international phenomenon. In 1932, Mickey's

overwhelming popularity was recognized by a special Oscar® awarded to Walt Disney for the creation of the world's most beloved animated character.

Mickey and Minnie's film careers took animation from a novelty to an art form of style and characterization. Mickey began to appear in color films and display previously unexplored emotional nuances. As a well-known public figure, Mickey eventually became less mischievous and more responsible than in his earlier films. Consequently, Disney introduced other cartoon characters, each possessing a different personality. Mickey, Donald, and Goofy teamed together in a series of shorts in the late 1930s. The comedy of this famous trio sprang from their contrasting characteristics, as well as from their individual reactions. So strongly defined were the supporting players—Minnie, Donald, Daisy, Goofy, and Pluto—that each became stars on their own. They played larger roles and became more essential to story lines; however, Mickey has never stepped away from his unofficial role as their leader.

In 1940, Mickey was cast in his first feature full-length film, *Fantasia*. By this time, Mickey was as red, white, and blue as Uncle Sam and the Statue of Liberty. To people all over the world, Mickey and the other Disney characters symbolized the American way of life. By the time that television became the predominant entertainment medium, Mickey and his friends had been in high demand on radio programs and in theaters for more than two decades. Disney became the first major Hollywood studio to enter the world of television with its 1950 Christmas special, *One Hour in Wonderland*.

Five years later, DISNEYLAND®, the world's very first theme park, opened its doors in Anaheim, California. That same year, *The Mickey Mouse Club* debuted, subsequently becoming one of the most popular children's shows ever aired. In 1961, Mickey and his friends burst forth in chromatic brilliance on *Walt Disney's Wonderful World of Color*, one of TV's early color series. The characters helped the Disney anthology become one of the longest running series in television history.

Mickey's fame and presence in the world remained strong in the decades to follow. The WALT DISNEY WORLD® Resort opened its doors in 1971, and since the Disney Channel began its premium cable service in 1983, Mickey and his friends have been delighting fans in the comfort of their own homes 365 days a year.

The characters that sparked a cultural phenomenon more than 80 years ago continue to inspire and entertain the world today. As they grace the pages of magazines and books, appear on toys and clothing, and entertain us in the theater and at home, Mickey, Minnie, Donald, Daisy, Goofy, and Pluto have become a part of our lives to a degree unequaled by any other cartoon or human character.

As the company grew, Walt Disney felt it was important to remind everyone of its roots and the necessity to stay true to them. In order to go forward with these characters and preserve their stature and longevity, we must get to know them, understand their origins, and trace their lifelong careers.

"I only hope that we never lose sight of one thing—that it was all started by a mouse…"   —Walt Disney

Tools & Materials

Before you begin drawing, you will need to gather a few tools. Start with a regular pencil, an eraser, and a pencil sharpener. When you're finished with your drawing, you can bring your characters to life by adding color with crayons, colored pencils, markers, or even watercolor or acrylic paints!

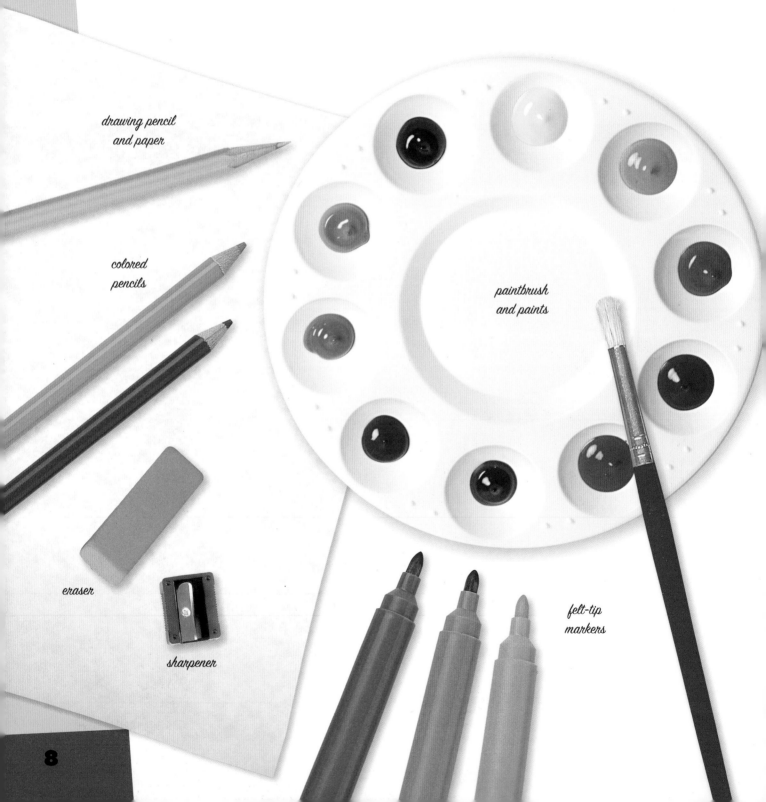

drawing pencil
and paper

colored
pencils

paintbrush
and paints

eraser

sharpener

felt-tip
markers

Getting Started

Usually artists draw characters in several steps. Sometimes the steps are different, depending on what you're drawing. The important thing to remember is to start simply and add details later. The blue lines show each new step, and the black lines show what you've already drawn.

Step 1

First you'll draw guidelines to help position the character's features.

Step 2

Next, you'll start to add details. It will take several steps to add them all.

Step 3

When you finish adding all of the details, you can erase your guidelines. Then you can darken your final sketch lines with a pen or a marker.

Drawing Exercises

Warm up your hand by drawing lots of squiggles and shapes.

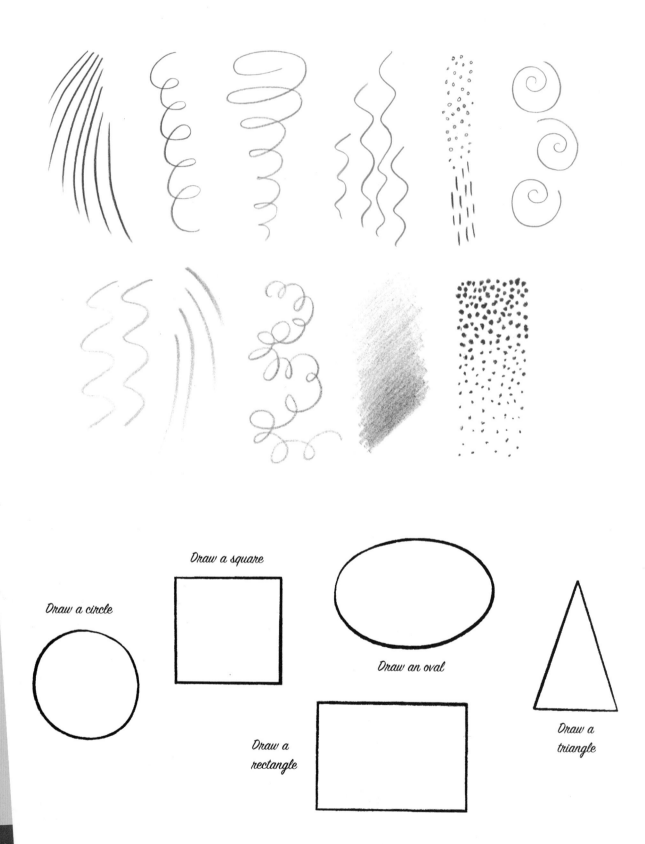

Draw a circle

Draw a square

Draw an oval

Draw a rectangle

Draw a triangle

If you can draw a few basic shapes, you can draw just about anything!

Circle

Ball

Triangle

Ice cream cone

Pizza

Sun

Square

House

Oval

Gift

Balloon

Submarine

Book

Rectangle

Truck

THE GANG

Size Chart

MICKEY MOUSE

Mickey Mouse is always friendly and outgoing. Everybody likes him.

MINNIE MOUSE

Minnie Mouse is Mickey's sweetheart and friend.

DONALD DUCK

Donald Duck has quite a temper, but he's still lots of fun to be around.

Check out how big (or small) the characters are compared to one another. When you draw them together, you'll want to make sure that you don't make Donald taller than Goofy! Remember that everyone is just about the same height except Goofy, who's the tallest.

Daisy Duck is Donald's favorite gal. She's quite fashionable.

Goofy is a pretty silly guy. Make sure you draw him having lots of fun.

Pluto is one happy pup! His best pal is Mickey Mouse, who also happens to be his owner.

MICKEY MOUSE

Mickey's Face

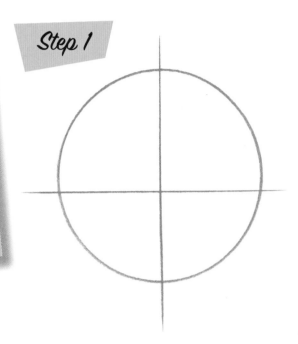

Start with a circle and guidelines.

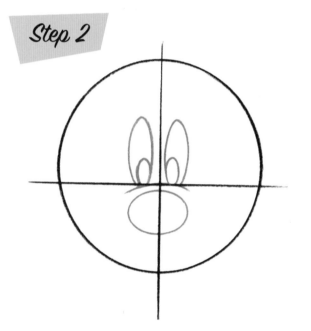

Add Mickey's eyes and nose. His eyes rest on the edge of one center line. Add a little curve right below his eyes.

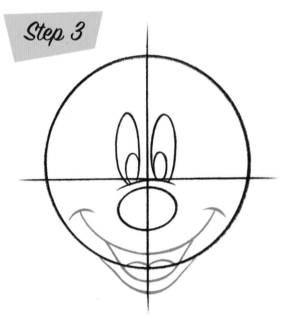

Add Mickey's smile and chin. The top of his mouth follows the same curve as his nose. Notice how his chin extends below the circle of his head.

Step 4

Draw two large ovals for Mickey's ears. Add curved lines to form the area around his cheeks and eyes. (This is called the "mask.")

Step 5

Erase your guidelines and clean up your drawing.

Step 6

Now add color!

MICKEY MOUSE

Mickey's Head

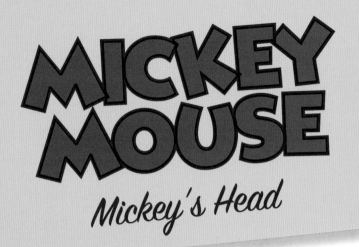

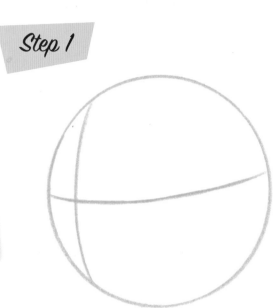

Step 1

Start with a circle and guidelines.

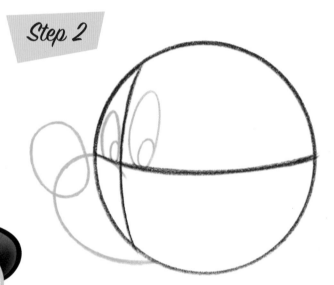

Step 2

Add Mickey's eyes and nose. His eyes rest on the edge of one center line. For his nose, draw a curved line for the snout. Position the bulb of his nose on the end.

16

"Mickey's a nice fellow who never does anybody any harm, who gets in scrapes through no fault of his own, but always manages to come up grinning." —Walt Disney

Step 3

You can always see both of Mickey's ears, no matter which direction his head is turned.

Add Mickey's smile and chin. The top of his smile follows the curve of his nose. Notice how his chin extends below the circle of his head.

Step 4

Draw two large ovals for Mickey's ears. In this view, one of Mickey's ears is on the top of his head, and the other is on the back. Add curved lines to form the mask.

Mickey Mouse has appeared in more than 130 film shorts, features, and featurettes.

Step 5

Erase your guidelines and clean up your drawing.

Step 6

Now add color!

Mickey's Expressions

tired

Mickey's eyebrows can show how he's feeling.

alarmed

When Mickey is surprised, his ears go up.

bashful

angry

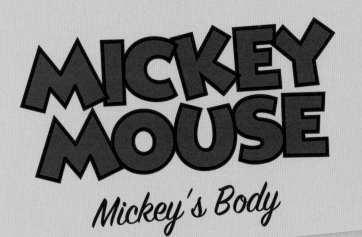

MICKEY MOUSE

Mickey's Body

When drawing the characters' bodies, notice the curved line going from top to bottom in Step 1. This is called the line of action. The line of action is a guideline to give your character direction and movement.

Mickey is 2-1/2 heads tall.

Step 1

Start with a circle for the head and a pear shape for the body. Draw a line of action down the center.

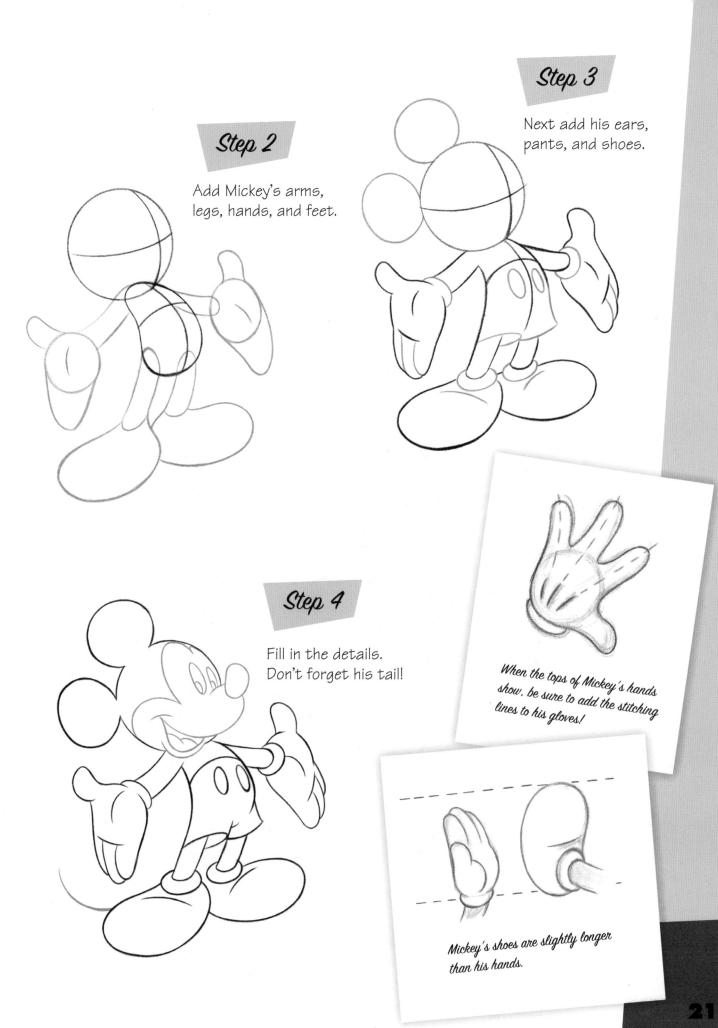

Step 2

Add Mickey's arms, legs, hands, and feet.

Step 3

Next add his ears, pants, and shoes.

Step 4

Fill in the details. Don't forget his tail!

When the tops of Mickey's hands show, be sure to add the stitching lines to his gloves!

Mickey's shoes are slightly longer than his hands.

Erase your guidelines
and clean up your drawing.

Step 6

Now add color!

22

Try these other poses of Mickey!

Minnie's Face

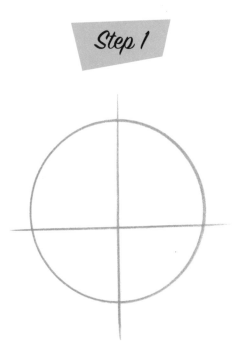

Start with a circle and guidelines.

Step 2

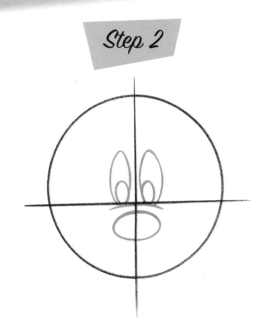

Add Minnie's eyes and nose. Her eyes rest on the edge of one center line.

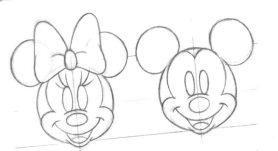

Minnie's head is similar to Mickey's, but Minnie's eyes are slightly larger and wider than Mickey's. Her open mouth is slightly smaller than his.

Step 3

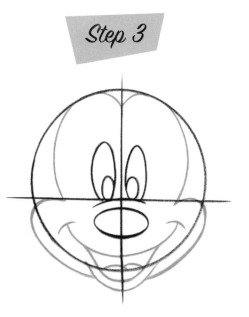

Add Minnie's smile and chin. The top portion of her mouth follows the same curve as her nose. Notice how her chin extends below the circle of her head. Add curved lines to form the mask.

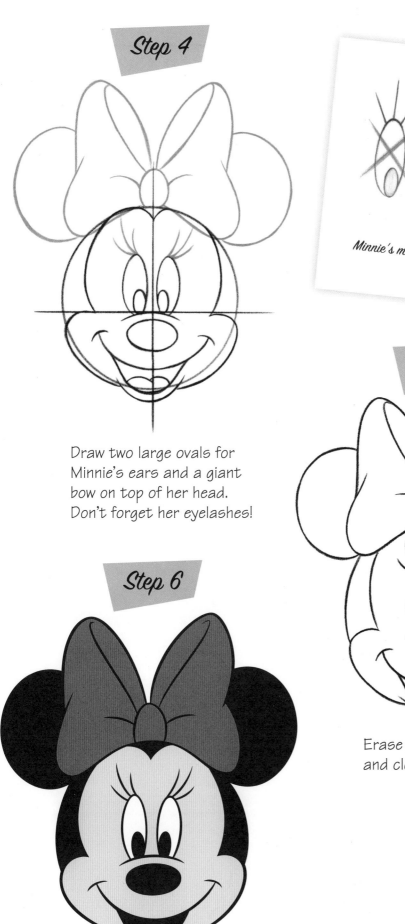

Step 4

Draw two large ovals for
Minnie's ears and a giant
bow on top of her head.
Don't forget her eyelashes!

Minnie's middle eyelashes are longer than the others.

Step 5

Erase your guidelines
and clean up your drawing.

Step 6

Now add color!

MINNIE MOUSE

Minnie's Head

Start with a circle and guidelines.

BETTER SHARPEN YOUR PENCIL FOR OUR EYELASHES!

Minnie and Mickey made their first appearance in the 1928 film short Steamboat Willie. They have since had one of the strongest and longest-running courtships in history.

Step 2

Add Minnie's eyes and nose. Her eyes rest on the edge of one center line. For her nose, draw a curved line for the snout. Position the bulb of her nose on the end.

Step 3

Add Minnie's smile and chin. The top of her smile follows the curve of her nose. Next add her mask and her eyelashes.

Step 4

Draw two large ovals for Minnie's ears. Don't forget her bow!

Step 5

Erase the guidelines and clean up your drawing.

Minnie is a fun-loving and nurturing friend, as well as a talented singer and dancer. She can be quick to scold when she feels slighted, but she is also quick to forgive and forget.

You can change Minnie's expression by tilting her head.

Step 6

Now add color!

Minnie's bow is large and full in form. It bends back slightly in profile or rear views.

MINNIE MOUSE

Minnie's Body

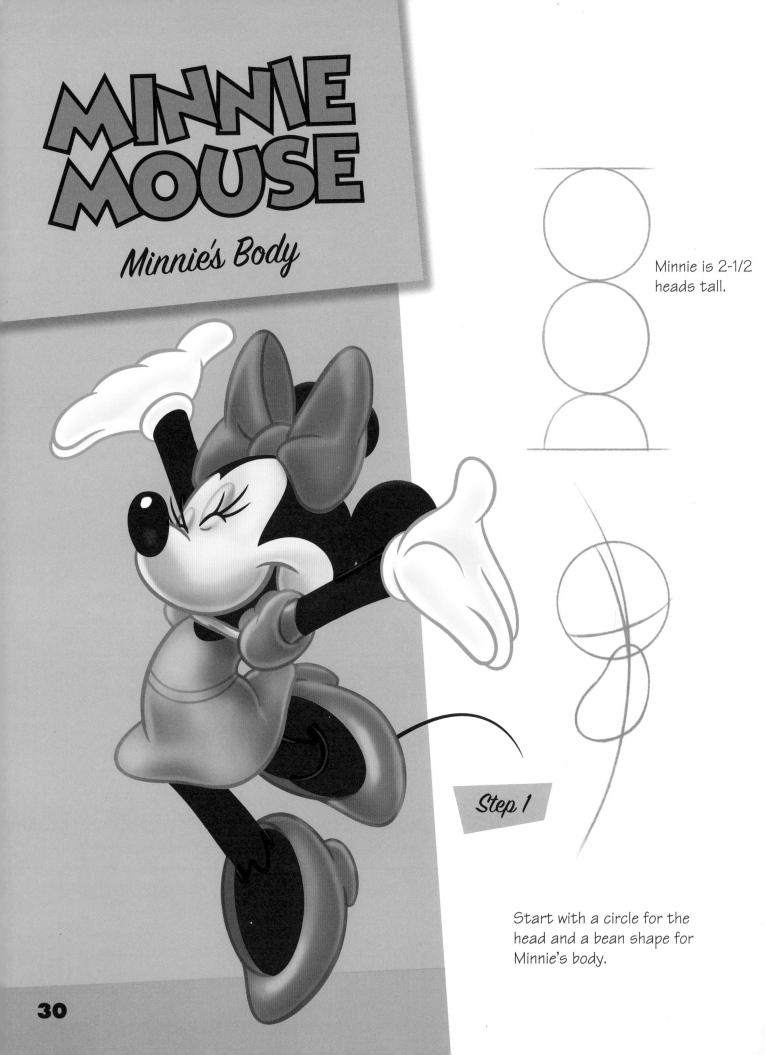

Minnie is 2-1/2 heads tall.

Step 1

Start with a circle for the head and a bean shape for Minnie's body.

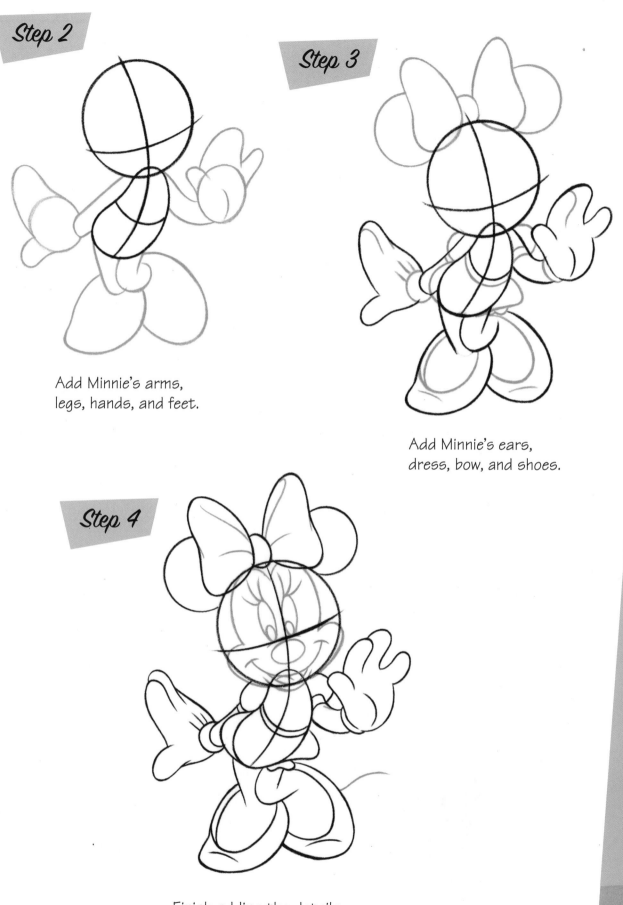

Step 2

Add Minnie's arms,
legs, hands, and feet.

Step 3

Add Minnie's ears,
dress, bow, and shoes.

Step 4

Finish adding the details.
Don't forget her tail!

Step 5

Erase the guidelines
and clean up your drawing.

Step 6

Now add color!

*Minnie's shoes have a wide, pointed
toe and thick, high heels.*

Try these other poses of Minnie!

DONALD DUCK

Donald's Face

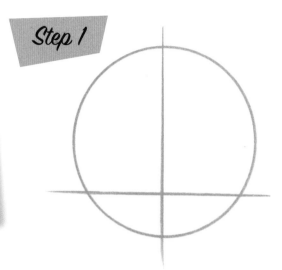

Start with a circle and guidelines.

Add Donald's eyes and the top of his bill. His eyes rest on the edge of one center line. Draw the curved lines for his bill.

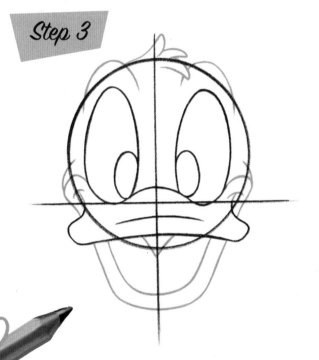

Add Donald's eyebrows and tufts on his head. Notice how his lower bill curves below his head. His cheeks are curvy when he smiles. Add a little triangle for his tongue.

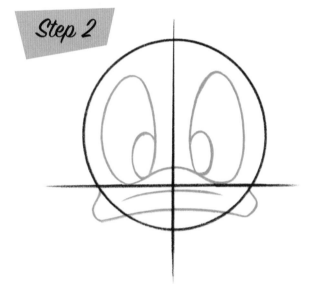

Step 4

Now add Donald's cap.

Step 5

Erase your guidelines
and clean up the drawing.

Step 6

Now add color!

Donald's hat is soft and flexible, but it always holds its shape.

DONALD DUCK

Donald's Head

Start with a circle and guidelines.

HEY! GO BACK TO YOUR OWN PAGE!

An overly confident duck, Donald's high opinion of his own talents often sends him chasing after the limelight, even if he's not the right candidate for the job. But despite his ways, it's hard not to like him.

Step 2

Add Donald's eyes and the top of his bill. His eyes rest on the edge of one center line. Follow the curved lines around the side of his head for his bill.

Step 3

Add Donald's eyebrows and tufts on the top of his head. Notice how his lower bill curves below his head. Now add a little triangle for his tongue.

Step 4

Add Donald's cap. In the side view, the ribbon on his cap falls to the back.

Step 5

Erase your guidelines and clean up the drawing.

Step 6

Now add color!

Donald's Expressions

mad

surprised

Donald's first performance was a supporting role in the 1934 film short, The Wise Little Hen, but he really let his feathers fly in the second film, Orphan's Benefit.

Donald's face changes when he's in different moods.

scared

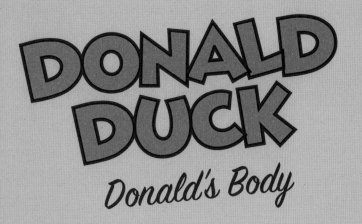

DONALD DUCK
Donald's Body

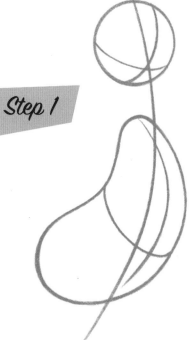

Donald is 4 heads tall.

Step 1

Start with a circle for the head and a jelly bean shape for Donald's body.

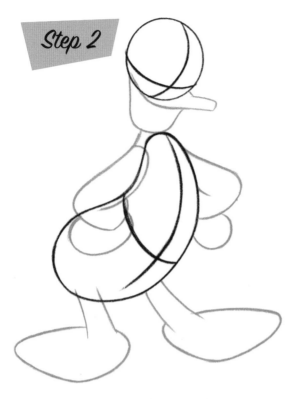

Step 2

Add Donald's arms, legs, hands, feet, and bill.

Step 3

Now add Donald's clothes.

Step 4

Donald's hands are almost as long as the height of his head.

Fill in the remaining details. Don't forget his tail!

Step 5

Erase your guidelines and clean up the drawing.

Step 6

Now add color!

Try these other poses of Donald!

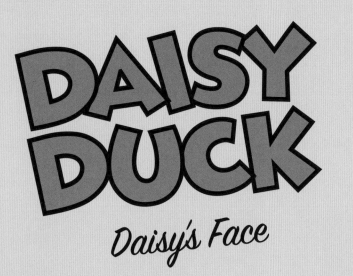

DAISY DUCK

Daisy's Face

Start with a circle and guidelines.

Step 2

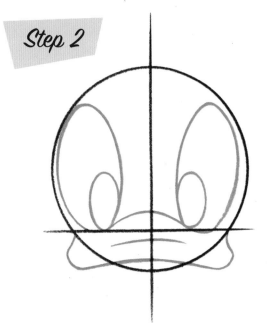

Step 3

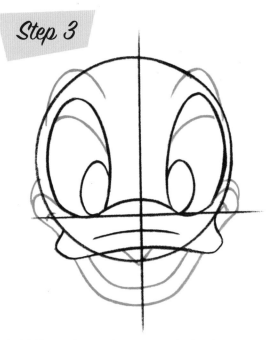

Add Daisy's eyes and the top of her bill. Notice how her eyes are rounder and more angled than Donald's. The bottoms of her eyes and the top of her bill fit together smoothly.

Add Daisy's eyebrows and the lower part of her bill. Now add the little triangle for her tongue, just as you did for Donald.

Daisy Duck is sassy yet sophisticated. She has impeccable manners and a passion for the finer things in life.

Step 4

Add Daisy's bow and eyelashes. She has three eyelashes over each eye. The middle lashes are longer than the others.

Step 5

Erase your guidelines and clean up the drawing.

Step 6

Now add color!

DAISY DUCK

Daisy's Body

Daisy is 4 heads tall.

Step 1

Start with a circle for the head and a pear shape for Daisy's body.

Step 2

Add Daisy's arms, legs, hands, feet, and bill.

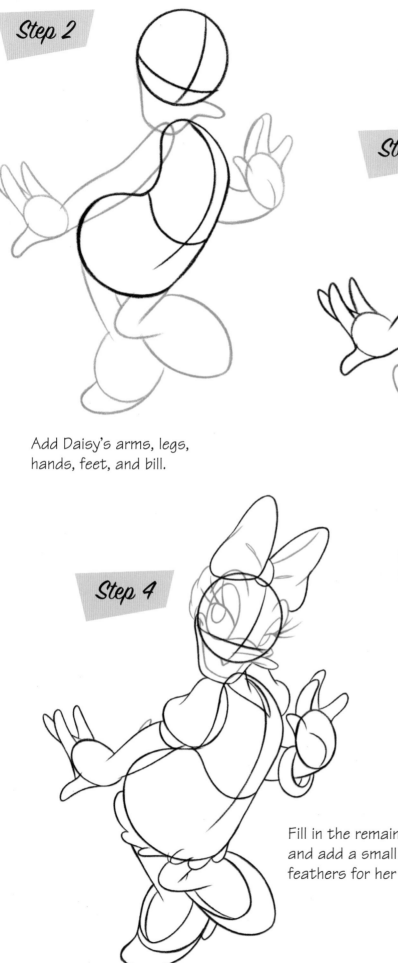

Step 3

Sketch in Daisy's clothes. Don't forget her bracelet.

Step 4

Fill in the remaining details, and add a small tuft of feathers for her tail.

Daisy Duck first appeared as "Donna Duck" in the 1937 film short Don Donald.

Daisy's bracelet hangs loosely from her left wrist.

Step 5

Erase your guidelines and clean up the drawing.

Step 6

Now add color!

Try these other poses of Daisy!

If you curve or tilt Daisy's body and head, she can look flirtatious, happy, or surprised.

GOOFY

Goofy's Face

Start with a circle and guidelines. In this drawing, part of Goofy's face is at an angle, so you'll make the center lines slightly angled too.

Step 2

Add a squished oval beneath the circle for Goofy's nose. Then add his cheeks, teeth, and mouth.

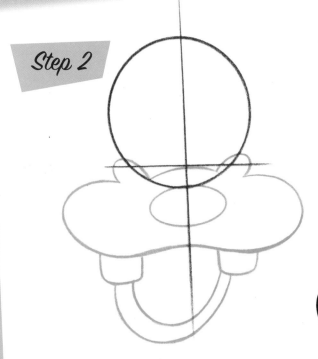

Step 3

Add Goofy's big oval eyes and tongue.

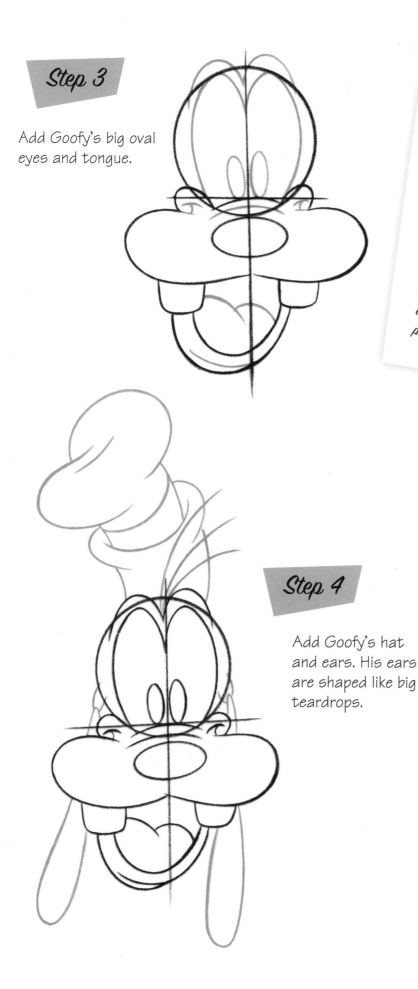

Notice how the whites of Goofy's eyes touch each other. Just make sure you keep his pupils separate.

Step 4

Add Goofy's hat and ears. His ears are shaped like big teardrops.

Goofy's head is similar to Pluto's.

Erase your guidelines.

Goofy's hat is about 1 head long. It's squishy looking and leans to one side.

Step 6

Now add color!

Goofy's high spirits and good humor are inspirational. No matter what chaos Goofy gets himself into, he always manages to come up smiling.

Goofy's Expressions

surprised

bashful

confused

Use Goofy's entire body to act out a mood or action.

GOOFY

Goofy's Body

Goofy is 8 heads tall.

Step 1

Start with a circle for the head and a banana shape for Goofy's body.

Step 2

Sketch in Goofy's arms, legs, hands, feet, and head.

Step 3

Add Goofy's clothes.

Step 4

Fill in the rest of the details.

Goofy first appeared in 1932 as "Dippy Dawg" in the film short, Mickey's Revue. Since then he has become known as a good-natured, happy simpleton with a heart of gold.

Step 5

Clean up your drawing.

Step 6

Now add color!

Goofy has BIG feet!

The toes of his shoes turn up slightly.

Try these other poses of Goofy!

Goofy's loose-limbed body is capable of a wide variety of poses.

PLUTO

Pluto's Head

Step 1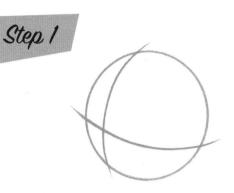

Start with a circle
and guidelines.

Step 2

Sketch in the snout and lower
jaw. Pluto has a long nose
pointing forward and a long,
rounded jaw dropping down
from the circle of his head.

Step 3

Add the details of
Pluto's nose and mouth.
Don't forget to add the
knob on the back of his head.

Step 4

Add Pluto's eyes. eyebrows, and tongue. Pluto's eyes are long ovals, and his tongue hangs down from his mouth. Now add his ear.

Step 5

Clean up your drawing.

Step 6

Now add color!

PLUTO

Pluto's Body

Pluto is 100% canine. Fun loving and playful, Pluto is full grown, but he has the spirit of a puppy. He is a loyal companion, always there for Mickey.

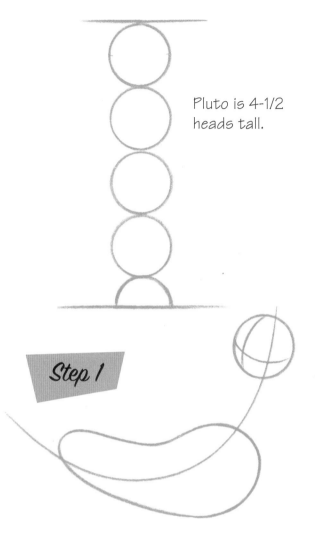

Pluto is 4-1/2 heads tall.

Step 1

Start with a circle for the head and a pear shape for Pluto's body.

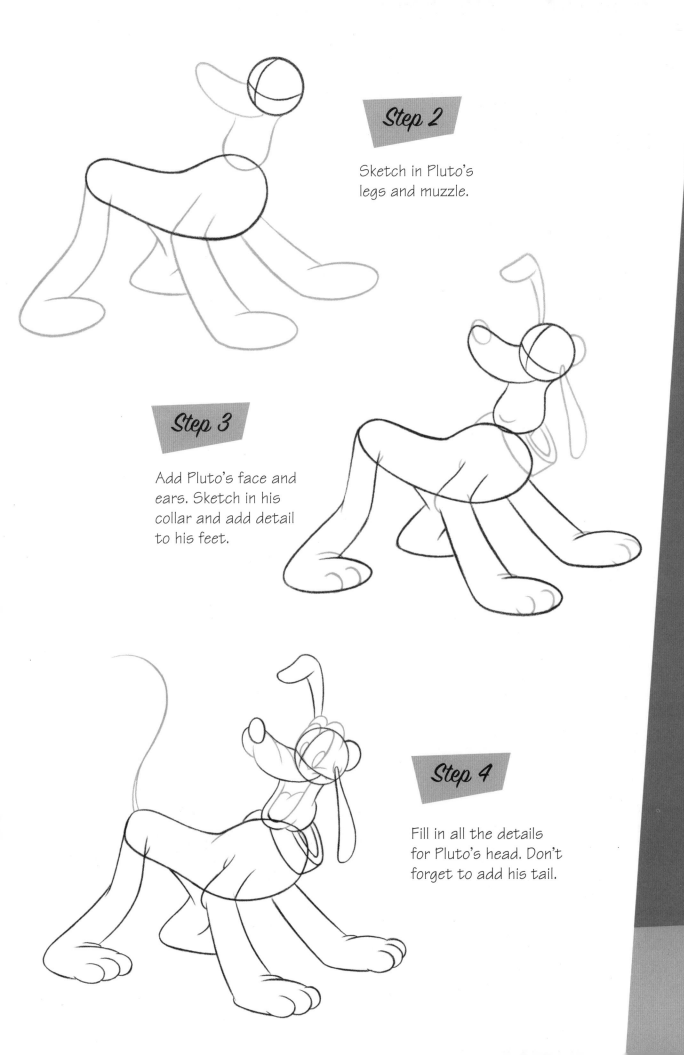

Step 2

Sketch in Pluto's legs and muzzle.

Step 3

Add Pluto's face and ears. Sketch in his collar and add detail to his feet.

Step 4

Fill in all the details for Pluto's head. Don't forget to add his tail.

His collar hangs loosely at the back of his neck.

Clean up your drawing.

Pluto's ears can act together to accentuate a mood or an expression.

Step 6

Now add color!

Pluto's Expressions

mad

stubborn

excited

Pluto first appeared in 1930 as an unnamed dog in The Chain Gang. The same year, he appeared as Minnie's dog in The Picnic. In 1931, he appeared as himself in the film short, The Moose Hunt. In 1941, Pluto gave an Oscar®-winning performance in Lend a Paw.

GOOD LUCK

Now that you've learned how to draw your favorite characters, try experimenting on your own. Remember to use your imagination—and have fun!